F*ck That

An Honest Meditation

F*ck That

An Honest Meditation

Jason Headley

THREE RIVERS PRESS · NEW YORK

Published in the United States by Three Rivers Press, an
imprint of the Crown Publishing Group, a division of Penguin
Random House LLC, New York.
www.crownpublishing.com

Three Rivers Press and the Tugboat design are registered
trademarks of Penguin Random House LLC.

This work has been expanded from the video "F*ck That,"
produced by the author, which first appeared July 6, 2015.

Library of Congress Cataloging-in-Publication Data
Names: Headley, Jason.
Title: F*ck that: an honest meditation / Jason Headley.
Description: First edition. | New York : Three Rivers Press,
2016.
Identifiers: LCCN 2015042223 (print) | LCCN 2015045671
(ebook) | ISBN   9781101907238 (hardback) | ISBN
9781101907245 (eBook)
Subjects: LCSH: Stress (Psychology)—Humor. | Meditation—
Humor. | BISAC: HUMOR / Form / Parodies. | HUMOR /
Topic / Adult. | HUMOR / General.
Classification: LCC BF575.S75 H43 2016 (print) | LCC
BF575.S75 (ebook) | DDC 155.9/042—dc23
LC record available at http://lccn.loc.gov/2015042223

ISBN: 978-1-101-90723-8
eBook ISBN: 978-1-101-90724-5

Printed in China

Book design by Elizabeth Rendfleisch
Cover design by Alane Gianetti
Cover photograph by vvvita/Shutterstock
Photograph credits appear on page 63

10 9 8

First Edition

For
and
thanks to
and
because of
Amy

Everyone who wills can hear the inner voice.
It is within everyone.

—Mahatma Gandhi

This book is a physical act of mindfulness.

By reading these words and turning these pages,
you will make your way to a more peaceful you.

Let's try it now.
Picture a thing that makes you
want to choke a motherfucker.

Now feel yourself release that thing
as you turn the page.

Just like that, there's no strife here.

Only a clear, calm place.

Turn the page again.

And feel the horseshit of the external world
fade from your awareness.

Let this meditation help you find peace
with the challenges that surround you.

Because they are fucking everywhere.

Am I right?

Here, you cannot be ensnared by anyone's dumbassery.

Not even your own.

If you find your mind wandering to other thoughts,
don't let it concern you.

Just acknowledge that all that shit is fucking bullshit.

Allow yourself to be lifted by the very best parts of you.

Leaving all the flightless shitbirds behind.

Where they fucking belong.

This is a new place in your life.
Clean and clear.

Free of calamity created by every last
ranch hand at the fuckup farm.

Those bitches can't get under your skin.

They can't even.

Take in a deep breath.

Now breathe out.

Just feel the fucking nonsense float away.

Breathe in strength.

Breathe out bullshit.

If your thoughts drift to the three-ring shit show of your life . . .

. . . bring your attention back to your breathing.

And with each breath, feel your body saying:

Fuck that.

Your thoughts become lighter.

And all the soul-eating cocksuckers
just fall away into nothing.

Let each turn of the page
guide you to a new place.

Away from lingering thoughts
about things you can't control.

Away from the soft whisper of doubt and concern.

Away from the cul-de-sac of useless fuckery
waiting at the ass-end of worry.

Simply turn each page.

To the next page.

Until the final page.

Where you greet the world and everything in it
with a new, beautiful breath . . .

. . . of fuck that.

Photograph Credits

ABOUT THE AUTHOR

JASON HEADLEY is a writer and director whose short films have been featured on the *Today* show, *SundanceTV*, and *Funny or Die* and in Banksy's Dismaland and film festivals far and wide. He is a participant in the IFP Emerging Storytellers program and a resident of the San Francisco Film Society's FilmHouse, and has also written, directed, and produced short films for Heineken, Sony, and Chrysler.

Meditate for up to fifteen minutes with the H*nest Meditation app.